MANAGER

How to be Successful in Your New Position

TABLE OF CONTENTS

INTRODUCTION

Congratulations on downloading *Manager: How to be Successful in Your New Position* and thank you for doing so.

The following chapters will discuss what to expect when you become a manager. It will explain the fundamentals of what being a manager entails. You will learn how to be an efficient communicator and to delegate responsibility to others. You will also learn how to handle mistakes and to listen to your employees.

There are plenty of books on this subject on the market, thanks again for choosing this one! Every effort was made to ensure it is full of as much useful information as possible, please enjoy!

WHAT TO EXPECT

A manager is simply just a title that is used within an organization to designate an employee that has obtained responsibilities to lead employees, departments, or functions. The manager has been assigned to a certain level within an organization. Employees that have a job title of manager have many different responsibilities to both function and people.

A simple job description for a manager differs within each organization.

The job description for a manager is at a classification level for a business that controls departmental success. A manager that is responsible for a certain will normally have employees that report directly to them.

Bigger companies might also have senior managers or managers that manage managers that report to a director or possibly a vice president. This will all depend on the size of the company.

The best description I can give would be that a manager has the responsibility for the work of a certain number of people.

A traditional definition says about the same thing: The manager has the responsibility for leading and watching over the abilities of the people under their command. What else could it mean and exactly what do they do?

Leading is the normal description for what managers do.

They are also responsible for leading a certain type of work, a functioning area, or a section of the company, either with or without a staff to report to.

Some organizations will have executive or senior managers that lead other managers that all have their own areas of responsibility and a direct reporting staff.

Some examples would be:

Tim is a marketing manager. He has six staff members that report to him. Tim is responsible for a section of the company's results, a functioning area market, and the six reports.

Suzie is the Human Resource manager. This is a functioning area and a sub-section of the company. She does not have any staff members that report to her but with the company's growth, she is planning on adding staff that will report to her.

Beth is the manager of event marketing and trade show. She manages the functioning areas of the show and the marketing for the events. She does not have and staffs and doesn't have any plans to get any in the future. She gathers resources from other people within the department that she is doing the event for.

Different department members will help her to staff and publicize the event. The graphics designer, the marketing communications writer, and the public relations manager, none of them report to her, but they could help her stage, market, and plan the event.

Stephanie is a senior manager for customer engagement. She has the responsibility for the results and work of four departments that make up the department of customer engagement. Within her role, all four department managers that report to her for their directions.

These managers have their own functioning areas: external development and training staff, administrative staff, technical support specialists, and customer service representatives.

Employees that have a title of manager, all have many responsibilities for functions and people. Each manager's job is unique, but they all have responsibilities.

Since the role of the manager has authority, accountability, and responsibility inside an organization, they have to do all of these.

Normally a manager's responsibilities will include:

Plan: Planning the functions and operations in an area where the manager has been assigned a responsibility so they can accomplish the goals that they are responsible for.

Implementation and organization: Organizing the resources that are necessary, training, workforce, and work, so that all the desired outcomes meet the goals.

Direct: They provide employees with resources and guidance, support, leadership, and direction that is necessary to make sure they can get the goals done.

Monitor: They follow through to make sure that the plans that were set forth to meet the goal are being done in a way to make sure that it is accomplished.

Evaluate: They assess and review the success of goals, plans, and how the employees are allocated with their resources.

They perform whatever responsibilities that get assigned to the by the director, vice president, or president or whoever the manager reports to.

These are normal roles of a manager:

1. Sets objectives: The manager will set goals for a group, and will decide what has to be done to meet the goals.

2. Organizes: The manager will divide the work into small manageable activities. They will select people to finish the tasks that have to be done.

3. Communicates and motivates: The manager makes a team from their people by making decisions on promotion, placement, pay and by communicating with their team. This is the integrating function that a manager will do. They mold their people into teams that cooperate well together so they can convey the information constantly around, down and up through the company.

4. Measures. The manager will establish correct yardsticks and targets. They interpret, appraise, and analyze performance so that the outcome will ensure the company is moving the right way.

5. Develops people: They do this by nurturing, training, and finding the right employees which are the company's main resource. This task is more important since the rise of the knowledgeable worker. Within this knowledgeable economy, people are a company's biggest and most important asset. The manager must develop this asset.

FUNDAMENTALS

It has probably been said about three million times but it still holds true today. Being a new manager is the most stressful role there is in business. From the new responsibilities to the new ways you have to relate to people. You are getting pressure from your management and your employees. It will feel chaotic.

Management is a complicated endeavor that requires a wide skill set. Mastering the fundamentals will provide you a solid foundation that you can build your everyday operations on.

Much too often, new managers just act as if their jobs are glorified contributors or worse, someone who just micromanages and works about two levels lower than what they should be doing. These are some basic ones and it is not an exhaustive list but these are some to help you get your year off to a strong start.

What is included in the list? Quite simply, a mix. A mix of business functions, behaviors, and skills that are called the fundamentals. These are key areas that you need to be conscious of and focus on when you start to sail into management for the first time.

Management is a vast ocean of subjects and there are many items that can be included on the list. These are the most useful:

Know your business: This one is as fundamental as can be. If managers don't know what functions they are supposed to manage, it will be a surefire recipe for destruction. Knowing what you are supposed to do will allow you to focus all your energy on where it needs to be and that is on managing others.

Take the time to know your employees: This is so basic but in is very often overlooked. If you want to have productive and loyal employees, you need trust and harmony. If you want to motivate your employees, if you want to know what they will respond to, you have to first understand them.

Communicate openly and often. This is an old cliché but it holds true. A good manager will be a good communicator. They need to provide guidance and feedback. A manager who doesn't like to communicate will find that the don't like managing. They are not going to be suited for it.

Make your employees' objectives measurable and clear. A manager's best friend is good employee objectives. All managers will provide a good map that will guide the employee's performance and will measure their results. These help to take the emotion and subjectivity out of the performance management and will turn it into more of a rational undertaking. In my personal experience, most managers I've known do not spend enough time with objective-setting.

Be comfortable with conflict: If you are in management for any length of time, you will figure out you have lots. It is best to not avoid it or steamroll it but just learn to deal with it diplomatically and fairly. Think of it as resolving instead of winning. Managing conflict effectively is a crucial skill that successful managers must have.

Emphasize accountability: Most managers including senior managers are weak when it comes to accountability. Holding employees accountable for their results is the mortar and bricks of management. If you don't hold employees accountable, chances are they will not produce the results you want.

Maintain credibility: Credibility is a priceless management asset. It is surprising how often management will shade the facts to suit their needs. They think that the upper management just doesn't get it. The truth of the matter is that they always get it. It is really common sense. Employees work the best and hardest for the ones they can believe and trust.

Start to think about developing your employees: It is never too early. Just like you appreciate it when others took an interest in helping to advance you career, your employees will appreciate it when you do it for them. It can make a world of difference in their attitude. Employee development is a crucial function for anyone in management but it is usually ignored but valued greatly if it isn't.

Ask for help if you need it: There is no shame in asking for help from senior managers if you need it. It makes perfect sense. That is a big benefit of working within an organization, help is very near. In early years of management, never hesitate to call colleagues, friends, mentors, other management or even human resources. You will not regret it. Adding perspective when you can't see the right answers is always the best option.

Lead by example: The quickest way to lose loyalty is to play by a different set of rules other than the ones you have set for your employees. It will alienate them very quickly. Walk the walk and going back to the trenches when you need to will set good examples that are easy to respect. It is an excellent way to be the kind of manager that others will follow.

When talking about management, fundamentals is always better than being fancy. There is absolutely nothing wrong with having presentation skills that can spellbind thousands. Chances are that operational effectiveness is determined by how you execute the fundamentals each day.

You need to be open to looking at things a different way. Great managers will be attuned, and flexible within their job. They will constantly be on the outlook for opportunities. Listen well. Many ways to change things will come for the people that work for you because they are the ones that are doing the work. Don't be afraid to move away from the ones who always want to do the same thing all the time.

Keep a high stand for excellence. You should have rules for excellence, and make sure your employees know you expect them to meet these rules. The good managers are ones that know how to get good work from their team, and not be being overly tough either. When your employees see that you have unwavering high standards, they are likely not to forget it. If they know that you demand excellence of yourself, they will find it within themselves, too.

You need to make sure that your employee's objectives reflect their abilities. Measurable and well-conceived objectives will be your best friend. They can move job performance from subjective to objective. If they are created with thoughtfulness first thing each year, they will work to guide you and your employees throughout the year.

Take care of time as if it were gold. Time is underrated but very critical as a management asset. It is important to the decision-making process. Leaders tend to get yanked in several different directions. This usually results in just barely getting things done instead of optimized work. Good executives would protect their schedules diligently. They would always do what needed to be done, but they knew how to prioritize and delegate very effectively which left them with time the think about what needed to be done.

Communicate and provide good feedback. Effective communication sounds a bit trite, bit it is because it is so fundamental to great management. Managers who are strong will be excellent at communicating. They will provide feedback which will include both negative and positive it is a core skill. Be available to the ones you manage. Even if you manage from home, you can still be reached easily by either text, email, phone, video chat, etc. It is best to be remote and easy to get a hold of, instead of being physically near but distant with communications.

Don't dodge conflict, deal with it fairly and directly. Any workplace is a place for conflict. Employee-management relations, cost-cutting, recognition, compensation, interpersonal issues, there will never be a shortage of emotionally charged problems that will lead to conflict. Even though it is tempting to look another way, the good managers will not be conflict avoiders. They will address the problems fairly and quickly. Employees notice everything. They take note on who will take action if they need to and who does not. Employees have respect for the managers that take on difficult situations. Just like they will lose respect for the ones who always avoids them.

Hire the best people. It literally starts here. If you have great talent, the rest will come easy. For reasons unknown, managers will take short-cuts when they are selecting, screening, and source their employees. Worse yet, the constantly rely on recruiters or human resources instead of seeing that selecting their own employees as a crucial part of their job.

Performance management is a large category that covers the aspect of people management within the manager's job. It will include setting and clarifying monitoring, measuring, coaching, goals, and expectations of the employee's work. They will also do performance reviews, develop training, coach, provide recognition and feedback, and address performance problems. It all depends on how many reports a manager has to do but this could take the majority of a week of the manager's time.

Developing their team. A manager has to develop a high performing team as well as managing and developing individual employees. A team the works together is more productive that individuals within a group that works independently.

Sets overall direction. Managers will set the short and long-term direction for the organization or team. This might include objectives, goals, missions, and visions or to simplify strategy. Strategic managers will spend most of their time thinking about the directions and missions. They are always looking for changes they need to make to reinvent their priorities. They, of course, will involve others that include their team. They will take all the responsibility for their final decisions.

Be a supportive and important team member. If there is a number one team, it needs to be your manager's, not yours. If there is any light between any of the executive team members, it will result in battles that cannot be won and the one that is lower on the corporate ladder are the ones who have to fight this battle.

Doing superb work that nobody should or could do. Almost every manager has their own responsibilities that they have to contribute to the team. It doesn't matter what level they are at. The higher up they are, the fewer of them there are. Chief Executive Officers even have things they have to do that they cannot delegate to others. They need to be careful that they are actually doing work that they can do and not just do things that they like to do. They don't need to do work just because they can't or don't trust their team to do or that they know they are good at.

Manage the resources. Managers need to make sure their team has what resources they will need to complete their work. They also need to make sure they team isn't wasting or overspending while doing so.

Improve quality and processes. While each individual employee needs to take responsibility for their own work, managers are in the position to see the complete workflow and then they can make the necessary improvements and adjustments.

Self-development. Managers aren't just responsible for developing their teams and employees, they have to development themselves as a manager, too. This includes reading about leadership and management, asking for feedback, seeking mentors, participating in management training, and developmental assignments. They are providing role models for improving constantly.

Communicate information. Managers will make sure that information comes from upwards, sideways, and above. They will never be the bottleneck of the information highway.

If you have ever wondered where leadership fits into all of this, it is woven through the entire process. Each of these need leadership to be effective. Leadership is never separate; it is always being.

You need to forget the word boss. The terms supervisor and boss were okay to use during the Industrial Revolution when it was clear that there were blue and white collar workers. Those particular words just don't hold true today. They don't accurately portray the role that you are doing. They might actually have more of a negative effect.

You might be better off using words like an advisor, obstacle-remover, team-leader, or chief-collaborator. Yes, these are all made-up words and they might seem a bit silly. And, of course, no one will ever address you by them. Your employees could just call you by your first name. If you can keep these terms in the back of your mind, they will keep you in the right frame of mind. Managerial roles were not made for people to boss others around. They were made to make sure that you and your employees work well together and as a team and as individuals so that you will be able to accomplish and exceed the goals that have been set. It will keep away resistance, but use the right amount of effort, talent, time, with just the right amount of compensation, praise, and recognition.

If you can keep the made-up words in mind, you will be able to think about your job in a more suitable workplace way:

- Collaborate with other members of your team. You engage with them to solve problems or create ideas. You're the top collaborator because you want cooperation yet stay accountable for how things turn out.

- As a team member, you have to be the example. Just like the pilot in a plane, you weave and coordinate the actions of your team to get the best results.

- You work to get rid of all obstacles like talent gaps, system inefficiencies, obstacles with customers, and issues within your department.

- You are an advisor for the people that work under you. You give the perspective on their weaknesses and strengths. You advise them on how to improve their skills and to excel. You advise them on ways to improve their work and skills so that they can excel.

- You are accountable for the team and you know that you are responsible for the outcome. You know that in the management world, you are the one that will be held accountable. You cannot throw your team under the bus. You will be accountable.

You must be truthful. That is extremely important. You are responsible for being truthful to your employees and co-workers. You need to expect them to be truthful with you as well. You will fail as a leader if you don't keep your integrity. Your main goal should be to share and gain respect and trust.

To quote Ralph Waldo Emerson, "Nothing astonishes men so much as common sense and plain dealing." This simply means that you are honest, open, and transparent with the way you have dealings with others. You can accomplish this by:

- You need to know yourself. Know your opportunities for growth, weaknesses, limitations, strengths, etc. Just be honest about all these when you are managing people and situations.

- You need to be truthful. You must tell the truth. You need to be tactful when talking about things that could be painful or even a surprise or could possibly offend others.

- You need to operate with clarity and integrity. Act and speak in a way that you can be very clear with your actions and words and give reasons for both.

- You must honor others. Have a presumption that everyone has worth and value and they are worthy of respect and civility. There have been managers totally upset their own effectiveness by disrespecting the other employees by gossiping, disrespectful words, or any other way they thought they could make themselves look better.

You need to show compassion. Compassion is a powerful tool for managers. You need to try to be in someone else's shoes and see things as they do. Ask people to tell you what might be going on they could influence how they act and work. Let them know you understand them. They might be feeling overwhelmed if they don't think they have the knowledge to do what has been asked of them. They may be feelings stretched a bit thin. Some may even feel underappreciated. Some might lack perspective. Or they are just stressed out and freaking out a bit.

To add compassion try:

- Empathize and listen to others. Try to go around a person's emotions by communicating with them to figure out what's wrong. Always think things through before you speak. Try your best to understand where they are coming from and then ask them to listen to your advice.

- Care about them. If you only care about yourself at work, you are causing yourself to have a hard time connecting to others. You won't be an effective manager.

- You need to share yourself. You may be able to help somebody with your own experiences. You can share your successes, failures, actions, or thoughts. Your experience might the thing that someone needs to hear to help them through a challenge. So share yourself humbly as you see appropriately.

- You need to admit your mistakes. If you can show a willingness to admit when you make mistakes, you will be helping your team to work through any problems they may have. They will be able to view you as a normal human and not a superior.

Your team needs understandable expectations. You need to have a fool-proof outline for what you are looking to achieve if you want your employees to do what you ask. There isn't anything more frustrating than figuring out that what you have been doing is not what they wanted from you. Set expectations for results and behavior. Communicate any praise or concerns through regular meetings. Here are some tips for setting some expectations:

- You need to do what you say that you are going to do. If you don't want to give any assistance, then tell them so.

Don't offer assistance than not following through. Never leave your employees in a lurch.

- You must model following through with your actions.

- You need to be clear about the outcome you expect. If you are discussing a task with an employee, you need to clearly state what you expect from them and then give them time to ask you questions about things they may not understand. Answer their questions or concerns honestly and clearly.

- Try to stay away from those last minute curve balls. If the task changes or anything about the task needs to be done differently, let them know as quickly as you can and give them the opportunity to adapt.

- You need to constantly demonstrate that you will honor a true effort. You might not always get the goals the way you thought you would. If the employees gave you their best effort, recognize their effort and examine what could have prevented your expected results.

- Please praise generously. You really just can't give enough recognition to your employees who are doing their best and actually a good job.

Try to keep your thoughts and feelings positive. A manager that goes down a road of negativity is taking a very dangerous path. If you constantly join in on bad comments that regards another department, a worker, another manager, or the company, you will lose all of the respect you have earned from your team over time. When you join in on the negativity about its systems, leaders, or the organization, you are modeling and promoting bad attitudes and behaviors.

You have to let your team know that you're on their side. You can do this without getting involved with all the negativity.

Listen to what they have to say and explain that you understand the problem. You need to find out how they want things to be fixed. You then, may attempt to talk to the other party, and then let them know what you have been able to do. By doing this you are building respect, trust, and confidence. You are also demonstrating true leadership instead of just being part of the group. Try being a leader by fixing problems in a good way. Show support by taking specific concerns to those higher up than you. You never discuss them with your own employees.

Becoming a manager is exciting. You get the chance to move upwards within a company. Along with this new job, you will discover new fears and responsibility. Know that all leaders and managers were in the exact same position as you at one point in their career. Find a mentor within your company whom everyone regards as a good manager. Take them to lunch or buy them coffee to get some sound advice.

EFFICIENT COMMUNICATION

You are a professional with enough expertise to be able to succeed in your field. You will have to eventually communicate with others that are either your peers or under your command.

Having communication skills become more crucial if you have been in your profession for a long time and have been fortunate enough to get promoted to a manager's position. You have more than likely received a wealth of information that you were not actually taught.

You need to communicate to be able to push projects through, but how we communicate now has changed. Email has wiped out the use of memos, faxes, and the common letter. Social media has even added another layer of communication that is very difficult to have control over.

What would the consequences of failing to communicate?

Well, your project or the client's need will not get met.

Your employees will be confused about what you expect from them.

The goals might come crashing down around all the heads of staffers, peers, superiors and yourself.

Not a pretty picture at all.

So, face it. Communication is in no way easy. Almost all professions will suffer from communication problems. About

70% of people that were asked stated that they never understood their accountant. Around 97% said they couldn't understand computer experts.

This miscommunication could be blamed on the facts that computer experts and accountants use a huge range of jargon and terminology.

Is what you do any different? Do you sleep well at night knowing that other people may not understand what you think of as crucial information? Is it easier knowing that whatever information you are passing on to others is actually getting through to them?

Here are some keys to be able to communicate effectively:

Speak briefly and clearly. Don't try to make your speech fluffy with big phrases and empty anecdotes. Cut down your words to the bare essentials and let the simple phrases do the lifting for you.

You need to back up ideas with a lot of knowledge. Make sure to stick to facts. Research goes a long way in proving the point and getting your audience's attention. If you can consider yourself an expert, you need to introduce yourself with your background information and then segue into your presentation.

Speak positively. Do not talk down to the audience or badmouth others within the profession. It doesn't matter if they deserve it. Taking the high ground will win you praise effectively and quickly.

Always think before you speak. You may use notes with most speaking occasions but if you practice it might be possible to not have to use a script. If you choose to go without a script, make sure you don't end up on a bridge to anywhere. You might not be able to find your way back, and you will lose your audience's attention.

Finish every single thought before you move on. This really shouldn't need an explanation but you aren't a good editor, vital information can be obscured.

Try to have a clear head and a calm attitude. Just like a pilot flies a plane, you need to know the best route to get from point A to point B. Stick to a certain route and get to the end of your voyage with applause.

By no means should you interrupt others. This is really important if you are on a panel discussion but is equally true for questions and answers. There is not a better way to turn people off than to interrupt their thoughts.

Some great speakers are just born but the majority of them have to learn. There is absolutely no shame in that.

You need to use the right communication tool. Most of the people who have to speak during meetings or at retreats have not been shown these tools or just never practiced them.

The good news is that these tools are easy to master, learn, and remember. What's better is that they will work in any situation. Whether it is formal speeches or just casual information sessions or perhaps a social occasion.

Employees absolutely must know how to communicate effectively to better understand each other and to have productivity in the workplace. Employees that have to do everything on their own are overburdened and will eventually fail to give their best.

Managers who can give effective communication helps the flow of knowledge and information among all the employees. Managers must interact with their employees to get the best from them. Problems will remain unsolved if the employees don't communicate with one another. Talking goes a long way in reducing confusions and improving the relationships amongst the employees.

Here are some tips to have effective communications within the workplace:

- Know that a manager is not supposed to just sit in a closed office and shout at their employees. They must interact with their employees regularly. Speak to your employees often. Ask them what they are up to. Treat them as one. There is no harm in taking your employees out to lunch. By doing this everyone is at ease and will talk about things more freely.

- Think about having morning meetings. Morning meetings help you to interact with your employees in an open atmosphere where everybody can express their views. Communicate with your employees and help them with their day. Let them tell you about their problems. Visit with them at their desks a couple of times each day.

- You need to learn to listen more. A good communicator will always be a good listener. It is very important to listen to others carefully before you speak. Interrupting conversations will break the momentum of the moment and the message will lose its impact.

- If you work as a team it will lead to better communication. Employees who work by themselves won't ever interact with other employees or superiors. Be sure your employees can talk to each other and work together. Make sure they know to let you know what is going on. Employees need to communicate with their managers to keep them in the loop on the latest developments.

- Be a master of writing emails. Train all your employees to write an official email. There is a big difference in a personal and official email. The subject line needs to let people what is in the email before they open it.

- Never call your employees one on one to any communications. You need to address them as a group.

- Always think before you speak. Make sure that what you are communicating is relevant. Don't use complicated words. The message needs to be precise and clear. Be sure to communicate clearly and straightforward as to what you want your employees to do.

- Communication is not complete until the message is completely understood by everyone. There is absolutely no room for anyone to be confused if there is good communication. When you have completed your speech, give the employees time to ask questions about anything they didn't understand.

- Don't try to communicate in a noisy place. Pick a meeting room, or conference room or anywhere it is noise free when you need to communicate.

A good manager needs to create a structure to be able to communicate at work. This may mean mapping out channels for every aspect of the business. Employees need to know who they have to go to get approval when they have completed a project. Employees need structure daily. Managers should tell them in advance when meetings are going to happen so that employees can prepare their questions. They need to talk with the employees about how much cooperation they need to use on a daily or weekly basis. They also need to get weekly reports from the employees about how well they performed and how well they expect to do the next week.

To create a true team spirit, managers need to lead their employees in solving any problems they have together. Managers that lead as dictators will stop the employees from using talents. They won't feel appreciated and won't communicate with a team. A good manager will seek input from their employees and will brainstorm to find solutions. This makes sure that employees feel like they are a part of solving problems.

Try to have strong visual communication. If you can present your data visually, it will help you communicate as a manager better. Tables, charts, and graphs will help people to understand the information immediately. Too much information in one image can make them confusing. Managers need to include just the most critical information in these images. This means they shouldn't add an image just to make the presentation look good.

Try to develop conflict management. Good managers will create a conflict- management policy to take care of conflicts before they even start. They will then communicate with employees so that they can take the responsibility of managing conflicts wisely. They must know how to listen well to alleviate conflicts. They should never, ever take sides. Letting the employees know that there is an open door policy encourages the employees to go to them for assistance.

Think about different cultures. Good managers need to understand the effects of communication with different cultural backgrounds. An employee that is from a different culture might take the manager's actions and words differently than someone within the same culture. Good managers will strive to learn what is acceptable and polite both nonverbally and verbally within the different cultures of their employees.

Work on their extroverted qualities. Managers have to try to communicate with confidence. They need to know when to be firm and when to relax. During a meeting with their employees, they need to make eye contact with each and every employee. They need to speak assertively. They need to keep a confident posture. They should speak with emphasis and not in a monotone voice.

Try to practice having strong written communication. Strong managers will strive to have well-organized, concise, and clear writing. They will also strive to keep the interoffice communication free from errors like inaccurate statements. Having strong writing will help employees see the manager as being a professional.

DELEGATE

How do you delegate? You start by letting the outcome you want to be known to people that you trust to get it done. Establish control and identify limits for the work and give support but oppose upward delegation. Stay up to date with the progress. Focus on the results instead of the procedures. When the work is finished, give the recognition that is deserved.

Everyone needs support and help. You should not feel ashamed if you need to ask for help. Put aside pride and show respect for other people's talent.

Remember there has never been a single-handed success. You need to acknowledge and include everyone that is on your team. You can propel your supporters, teammates, and yourself to great heights.

If you feel overloaded or stressed, or your career seems to be stalled, you might need to dust off your delegation skills.

If you are self-employed, then there is a limited amount that you can do. It doesn't matter how hard you work. There are only so many hours in a day that you can work. You can only complete so many tasks in said hours. There is only so many people who can help you with these tasks. Your success will be limited since the number of people that you can help is limited.

If you are good at what you do, then people will want a lot more from you. This could lead to work overload and pressure. You absolutely cannot do what everyone wants you to do and this could leave you unhappy, stressed, and feeling as if you have let people down.

You have been given a great opportunity if you can get around the limitations. You will be successful if you realize the opportunity.

The best way to overcome this limitation is learning how to delegate work to others. If you can do that well, you could quickly build a successful and strong team that is able to meet the demands of others. This is the main reason delegation is a great skill and one that you must learn.

So why doesn't people delegate? You must first understand the reason why people avoid it. Simply, people don't because it just takes too much effort.

What is easier, writing and designing the content for a brochure that will promote a service that you helped to spearhead, having others do it? You know it's content frontwards and backward. You can say its benefit statement while you sleep. It would be easy for you to just sit down and write it. It would be so much fun. The big question is, would you be using your time well?

On the surface, it would be easier for you to do it by yourself instead of trying to explain the strategy of the brochure to anyone else. There are two main reasons that will mean it would be better to delegate it to another person:

First of all, you have the knowledge to start up a new campaign. Chances are your skills would be better used to develop a strategy and come up with new ideas. By doing it yourself, you will be failing to make good use of your time.

Second of all, by involving other people, you will develop their abilities and skills. That means the next time another project comes along, you will be able to delegate with confidence that it can be done well with less work from you.

Delegating allows you to use your skills and time for the best and it will help others to develop and grow to the full potential within the organization.

When is the right time to delegate? Delegation is best when done appropriately. That doesn't mean you can delegate everything. You must figure out when delegation would be most appropriate. Here are five questions you need to ask:

1. Is there anyone else who can be trusted with the information and who has the expertise to finish the work? Can this task be done by someone else or is it crucial that you do it?

2. Will this task provide someone else the opportunity to develop and grow their skills?

3. Will this task recur in the near future?

4. Will you have the right amount of time to effectively delegate the job? There needs to be ample time to train, to ask questions and get the answers. Will there be an opportunity to check on progress and to do rework if necessary?

5. Should I delegate this task? Tasks that are crucial for success in the long run really do need your full attention.

If you answered yes to some of the above questions, then it would be well worth your time to delegate this job to someone else.

A couple quick tips to consider that can contribute to the task getting delegated:

- The deadline for the project:
    - Is there enough time to do the job?
    - Would there be time to do the job again if it didn't get done right the first time?
    - What happens if the job doesn't get done on time?

- The goals and expectations of the project will include:
    - Do the results need to be the highest quality?
    - Will adequate results be good enough?
    - Would failing be critical?
    - How would failing affect other aspects?

With all that said, if all these conditions are present there is no guarantee that the task will get completed successfully. You will also need to think about who you will delegate the task to and how to do it.

How to delegate and who to delegate to? Once you have decided to delegate a task there are a few factors that you have to consider.

First off, to whom do you delegate? The factors that you need to consider are:

1. The skills, knowledge, and experience of the person as they start on the delegated task.
    a. What is the attitude, skills, and knowledge of the person?
    b. Is there resources and time to give them training if they need it?

2. The person's work style.

    a. Is the person independent?

    b. What do they want out of their job?

    c. What are their interest and goals, and how do they meet up with the proposed work?

3. What is the workload of the person?

    a. Will they have time to do another task?

    b. If you delegate this task, will you have to shuffle other workloads and responsibilities?

You might notice that they will take longer to complete the tasks than you do. This is due to the fact that you are an expert and the person you delegated is still learning. Just have patience. If you have made the correct decision and communicated with them right, you will soon figure out they will quickly become reliable and competent.

So, how should you delegate? Use these tools to delegate successfully:

1. Clearly, let them know the desired outcome. Start with the end and specify all results that are desired.

2. Identify all boundaries and constraints. Can they take upon themselves accountability, responsibility, and authority? Should they:

    a. Wait until someone tells them what to do?

    b. Ask what they need to do?

    c. Act first, then report the results immediately?

    d. Confirm what needs to be done and act?

    e. Take action and report in periodically?

3. If at all possible, include others in the delegation process. Let them decide what tasks need to be delegated and when.

4. Make sure the amount of responsibility is equal to the amount of authority. Know that you can delegate responsibility, but you can't take away the accountability. The buck will always stop with you.

5. Delegate to people on the lower levels. People who know the work will be the best to do the task since the have the knowledge of the work. This will also increase efficiency within the workplace. It also helps to develop people.

6. Provide support and be there to answer any questions. Make sure the project will succeed by communicating and monitoring and provide them with resources and give them credit.

7. Stay focused on the results. Think about what has been accomplished instead of harping on how the work needs to be done. Your way may not be the only way or the best way. Let them control their own processes and methods. This will show trust and success.

8. If a problem arises, don't allow them to shift the responsibility back to you. Ask them for solutions and don't just give them the answers.

9. Build their commitment and motivation. Talk about how their success will result in good consequences, informal recognition, other opportunities in the future, and even financial rewards. Give recognition where it is deserved.

10. Maintain and establish control.

    a. Talk about deadlines and timelines.

b. Everyone involved will need to agree on the schedule for checkpoints where you will review their progress.

c. Make any adjustments as needed.

d. Take the time to review all the work that has been submitted.

When considering these points thoroughly during and prior to the delegation process, you will soon find that you can delegate a lot more successfully.

Make sure you keep control. When you have worked completely through the steps, be sure to talk to your employees appropriately. Take the time to explain to them why they were chosen, what is going to be expected from them, the goals you have set, the deadlines, timelines, and resources that they can use. Agree upon a schedule for checking in with updates.

Make sure they know to let you know of any problems that occur. They need to know that you are available to talk to if they have any questions or need guidance as the project continues.

We know that managers don't usually micromanage but this doesn't mean that we must control everything. When we delegate effectively, we must find the correct balance in giving the space people need to be able to use their abilities effectively while supporting and monitoring enough to make sure the job gets done effectively and correctly.

When the delegated work gets delivered back to you, take enough time to review it completely. If it is possible, only accept quality, complete work. If you take work that you are not completely satisfied with, your employee did not learn how to do the job correctly. Worse yet, you have just accepted a portion of the work that you will have to finish yourself. This overloads you and you won't have to time to do your own work well.

When you get good work back, make sure to reward and recognize the effort. As a manager, you need to practice complimenting your employees whenever you are impressed with what they do. This will go a long way toward building their efficiency and confidence. Both of these will improve with the next delegated task therefore, you both are winners.

Some key points to remember:

At first, delegation might feel more like a hassle than what it is worth. But if you can learn to delegate effectively, you can expand the amount of work you can do by a lot.

If you can arrange the workload so you are working on tasks with the highest priority, and others are working on challenging and meaningful assignments, you now have a recipe for huge success.

To be able to delegate effectively, pick the right tasks to delegate. Find the right people to delegate to. Delegate the correct way. There is a lot to this, but you will achieve a lot more when you learn to delegate effectively.

HANDLING MISTAKES

Being a manager, you might find that the scariest thing you've had to do is to let your employees make mistakes. Your employees will grow when they make mistakes. A good leader will fix things so that their employees can take risks. All managers want to help their employees to grow. As Meg Cabot once said, "Courage is not the absence of fear, but rather the judgment that something else is more important than fear".

The first step is determining the areas within the business where are mistake won't cause a lot of problems. Make sure that the areas where clients trust could be hurt would be off limits. Identify areas where employees can have the freedom to look at different ways of handling problems.

The next thing is to let your employees know that there is going to be an official policy such as: Making a mistake once is fine as long as it was a mistake made during the attempt to accomplish something they thought was right. They can make a mistake once but making the same mistake twice is not okay. The main rule is when you make a mistake for the first time; the team will be there to help. If you repeat the mistake twice, then you are 100 percent fixing it on your own. This rule applies to all first-time occurrences for each new mistake.

Everybody makes mistakes. If mistakes aren't made, then new things aren't being done. John Wooden once stated, "If you're not making mistakes, then you're not doing anything". New ideas and innovations happen through mistakes. You area able to step outside of your comfort zone when you make mistakes, and then you will discover new things that you didn't before you made the mistake. Don't look at mistakes as failures; they are just a way of eliminating things that don't work so we can come closer to what will.

Great managers will let their employees make mistakes. An employee that learns from their mistakes is a great employee. They take responsibility for them and will fix them. They create rules to make sure that those mistakes won't ever be repeated.

To break each of those down:

1. Grow from your mistakes: The best employees will know when they've made a mistake. They don't try to deny their mistakes. They see their mistakes objectively and see what went wrong. They understand why their actions were wrong.

2. They own their mistakes: They are always accountable for all mistakes they make. They don't come up with excuses and they don't try to hide them. They will inform others of things they have learned from the mistake that they have made.

3. They fix their mistake. Good employees will do whatever it takes to fix their mistakes. There may be times when too much damage is done and they can't change that but good employees will do the best they can to fix the damage. They will establish a timeline and follow up with the progress so everyone feels the care and urgency that is being put into fixing the problem.

4. They will put safeguards in to make sure the same mistakes aren't repeated in the future: This is the most important part of learning. When there has been a mistake, it's important to figure out what you can do to keep that same mistake from being made again. Take notes so lessons that were learned can be passed down to

other employees. Do whatever you can to make sure other people don't end up making the same mistakes. Share your new found discoveries.

These steps apply to all areas of life. It doesn't matter if it is personal, home, or business these principles will always be the same. The good employee will have mistakes, but a great employee will know how to apologize for making the mistake.

A great employee will know all the A's for a good apology:

You must ADMIT the mistake.

You need to APOLOGIZE for the mistake.

You will ACKNOWLEDGE where the problem happened and notice what exactly when wrong.

You will ATTEST to the mistake and plan on fixing it within a certain timeline.

You will ASSURE that you have put protection in place so you won't make the same mistake twice.

You will ABSTAIN from making the mistake again.

Employees who can implement these A's will discover that the respect they earn from others will grow. People that live by the A's will be forgiven quicker by others, and they will be willing to let them have a second chance. Making a mistake isn't ever the problem; it's how you respond to the mistake that counts.

Oscar Wilde once said, "Experience is the name everyone gives to their mistakes".

It has often been said that mistakes will provide a great learning opportunity. It would just be better to not make any mistakes at all. Let's look at the ten most common mistakes that managers make and see what you can do to stay away from them.

Learning about these now instead of through experience, you can save yourself the trouble.

1. You are not providing enough feedback. Becky is a good sales rep, but she has a bad habit of answering the phones very unprofessionally. Her boss knows the but is waiting for the performance review to let her know. The bad thing about this is that if she isn't told about the problem, she doesn't know she needs to fix the problem. She will just continue to make potential customers mad.

    Failing to provide feedback is a common mistake that managers can make. If you don't provide good feedback, you are depriving your employees the opportunity of improving their performance.

2. You are not making time for your employees. If you are a manager, it can be easy to get wrapped up in your workload that you aren't available to your employees.

    Yes, you have your work to finish, but your employees need to come first. If you aren't available when they need you, your employees will not know what they are supposed to do. They will not have the guidance and support they need to be able to meet their objectives.

    To avoid this mistake by blocking time in your daily schedule for your employees and learn how to listen to them. Develop emotional intelligence so you can be more aware of your employee's needs. Have an open door policy at certain times so your employees know when they can talk with you. You can always take the time to visit your employees at their desks.

    When you are in a management role, your employees should always be first. This is exactly what good management is about.

3. You do not need to be too hands-off. One of your employees just finished a big project. They misunderstood the specifications of the project and you didn't check in on them as they were working. Now, the project has been done the wrong way and you have to explain to an angry client what went wrong.

   Most managers try to avoid micromanaging. Going with hand-offs is not a good idea either. You have to find the correct balance.

4. A good manager won't be too friendly. Most managers want to be approachable and friendly to their employees. People are happier when they work for someone they like. You might find that it is hard to make tough decisions regarding your employees. Some employees might even be tempted to take advantage of you when you are too friendly.

   Now, this doesn't mean you can't talk or socialize with your employees, you just have to get the right balance between friendship and being the boss. Make sure you implement clear boundaries so your employees can't take advantage of you.

5. You fail to define their goals. If your employees don't know what their goals are, they will just shuffle through the day. They won't be productive if they don't know what they are working toward, or what their work even means. They can't prioritize their workload and this means that tasks or projects won't get completed in the right order. Avoid this by setting goals for your employees. Use a chart to specify where the employees should be going and show them the resources they can use. Use objectives to align the employee's goals to the company's mission.

6. Your employees misunderstand your motivation. Do you have any idea what motivates your employees? It is probably not just money. Most managers make a mistake by assuming their team is just working for money. It is not likely that this is all that motivates them.

    Employees that seek a greater life/work balance could be motivated by days they can telecommute and have flexible schedules. Some might be motivated by achievements, praise, extra responsibility, or just for the camaraderie.

7. You can't hurry through recruitment. If your employees have a huge workload, you need to have enough people to be able to get it finished. If you fill a vacancy too quickly could be a huge disaster.

    Hurrying up the hiring process can lead to hiring the wrong person. They might be unproductive, ineffective, or uncooperative. They may need more training and will slow down the other employees. With the wrong people, you will be wasting time and resources if they don't know what they are doing or if they get frustrated and leave. What makes this worse is your other employees will be frustrated and stressed by having do the work of the new employee. You can easily avoid this by knowing how to hire effectively and being picky about who you hire.

8. You are not walking the walk. If you like to make personal calls during work or you speak negatively about your boss, do you really expect your employees to not do by your example? Absolutely not.

    As a manager, you must be a role model for your employees. That means if they must work late, so do you. If the company has a rule of no eating at your desk, then set an example and go to the break room at lunchtime. If you have a bad attitude, your employees will have bad attitudes.

Your employees are watching everything that you do. If you want their behavior to change, start with yours. They will follow you.

9. You are not delegating. We talked about delegating in the last chapter. Some managers just don't delegate, because they feel like nobody can do the job the way they can. This will cause large problems because the work will bottleneck as they get burned out and stressed.

   The delegation will take some effort up-front. It might be hard for you to trust your employees to do the job right. But if you never delegate tasks, you will never have the time to focus on the big stuff that managers are responsible for. You will fail to help your employees develop new skills so they can take some of the pressure off of you.

10. You might be misunderstanding the meaning of your role. When you become a manager, the responsibilities you have will be a lot different from the ones you had before.

    It might be easy for you to forget that your objectives have changed and you now must use different skills to be effective. This will lead to you not doing what you were hired to do which is managing and leading. You will fail if you just rely on your technical skill by themselves, it doesn't matter how good they may be.

Here are some key points to keep in mind:

We are human, therefore we will make mistakes. There will be certain mistakes that managers will make in particular. These will include misunderstanding your role, not delegating effectively, being too hands-off, and not give feedback.

While it is true that mistakes could be an opportunity to learn, you need to take the time to recognize and try to avoid common mistakes. This will help you to become more successful and productive. You will also be respected by your employees.

LISTEN

If an employee says they want to be heard, what they are really saying is they want their managers to not just hear them but to listen to them. When employees want more support, feedback, and attention, managers must be more in tune with what their employees need so that they can be a more effective manager. Managers who listen can create a trustworthy relationship that will breed loyalty. You have known managers who always has the employees backs because they really and truly listen to them.

When you are a manager, it may be difficult to figure out what an employee thinks. You have no way of knowing what is troubling them or even how to get them out of their slump. You can't unless you start listening. When you listen, it's more than just listening to them fully. You must be aware of their natural tendencies, mood, facial expression, and body language. Listening is a job itself if you think about all the uncertainty that is found within the workplace and all the changes that happen.

As managers, you have to balance our desire and intensity to be able to perform with compassion and the attention that your employees deserve. Take notice of other's tension and emotions before it has a chance to impact your work; makes you have to up your emotional intelligence.

You won't find listening on the typical job description. The ones who can listen are in the best candidate to control the workforce. The one-size-fits-all thinking is outdated. The ones who can understand and practice the art of listening will turn out to be better, more compassionate and understanding leaders.

Here are some ways to listen that can help you:

1. You show your employees you care. Employees that feel cared for will work better. Employees want a leader who cares who they are and what they bring to the company. Don't view the people that work for use as tools to help you succeed. They are people that all have different attitudes and abilities that are not limited to just the functions of their jobs.

    Many managers have said that their relationships with their employees stay with work. That kind of relationship will be short-lived. Employees are looking for leaders that will take time to get to know them, and care about them professionally and personally.

2. You have to be engaged. There's more than just engaging and caring about the things that are most important to the employees. If an employee wants to share a thought, engage them, and ask questions about it so that they can elaborate on their thoughts. If you can learn to follow up with employees, keep accountable, and engage yourself more, it will show your employees that you are truly paying attention, listening, and trying to understand and relate to them.

    I had a manager who told me I had a rare way of giving my opinions during meetings. They didn't try to change me into something or someone I wasn't but embraced my way and used it to stimulate meetings. There were times they wanted me to lead the meetings if he had to do something else. He always made me feel like he was listening because he would apply what he learned about my style. I was eternally grateful for having this compassionate manager as my boss since he gave me the incentive to be myself.

3. You must be empathetic. Work is a place full of pressure and stresses each and every day. Each employee will manage pressure and stress differently. You need to be empathetic to how these impact your employee's performance.

    Express concern and show them that you understand their frustrations. If you have been in your management position for a long time, it might be hard for you to express or feel sentiment because you are afraid it will weaken your authority.

    Empathy is a great way to display that you are listening. Many managers try to avoid interactions that involve emotions but the best managers will know how to make themselves available to the ones who need their attention. There were two presidents that were great at showing empathy to others and they were Ronald Reagan and Bill Clinton.

    Great managers will know how to have a balance between the heart and the head.

4. You must not judge others. Managers that tend to judge their employees aren't really listening. There are times that leaders make bad criticisms about employees that have different ways of doing things. They should be learning from them instead of judging them.

    Managers expose their inability to embrace differences and immaturity when they judge. They might have a long track record with one company but will find it hard to make a transition to a new company.

Managers do not need to grow content. Managers today must embrace new ideals and ideas. They have to be active listeners, adapting to change and constantly learning.

5. You must be expansively mindful. Great managers will be extremely mindful of what is around them. They will know how to listen beyond the obvious non-verbal and verbal communication. They can recognize others through nods, facial expressions, and body language. These managers possess a huge degree of managerial presence. They are tuned into everything that is going on around them all the time.

   Managers that stay mindful are not hearing the conversations. They are engaging in dialogue as well as listening. They are never faking it. They are taking notes on what is being said and how it is being said. They are continuously making gestures and eye contact.

   As a manager, everybody is watching everything that you do. If you look as if you are disconnected, people will perceive you as not listening and disinterested. Don't ever stop being mindful.

6. You don't interrupt anyone while they are speaking. How many times have you been interrupted while talking and it totally ruins your thought process? It's easy to say that this is a common occurence. Compassionate managers will listen without interrupting. They will embrace communication and are aware that every time they interrupt there will be disengagement. They always earn respect by being a patient and great leader.

Managers need to stay focused on what others are saying. Be respectful of others and stay in the moment. Listen well and be a caring leader.

Employees have more respect for mangers that listen to them. They know that listening can be difficult.

These are some statistics that shows how important listening is:

- About 85 percent of all your knowledge, was learned with listening.

- People will comprehend about 25 percent of what they hear.

- During a normal day, you spend 45 percent of the day listening, 30 percent communicating, 16 percent reading, and the last 9 percent writing.

- Only two percent of professionals will have formal education to learn to improve, understand, and improve their listening techniques and skills.

The best manager I worked under would always come around their desk when any of us needed to speak with them. When asked why they responded by saying they thought that sitting beside the person instead of behind their desk lead to better discussions. They are putting their employees at ease. They are conveying they genuinely care about the employee, and they are intently listening to what the employees have to say.

They have made listening to a priority. They can tune into the person that is speaking and have an open mind without seeking conclusions or try to problem solve while the employee is speaking. It was noticed and admired many times, not just be their employees but by the senior executives as well. Many managers are learning just how important listening is today.

So why now? Why are managers striving to better their listening skills? Because the quality of our influence is dependent on how well we listen and all this brings many benefits to the company.

Consider the fact that about 40 percent of people who work do not feel appreciated or valued. About 70 percent of them are actually looking for another job or would accept the first offer that came their way. Now is the time we need to be reaching out to our employees in very meaningful ways.

Email has become the quick and easy way to answer questions, make requests, share info, and communicate. There is a very dark side to all these emails that come to us. First, it all depends on how disciplined we can manage emails. You may have between 100 and 300 emails daily that you have to read, respond to, delete, or act on every day. The most disturbing fact is that emails have actually replaced conversations.

We just don't take the time to connect and maintain good relationships with people around us like we should. We are constantly going from the time we open our eyes each morning until we close them at night. We are just too busy.

We have to remedy this situation if we deeply care about our employees and their success. We have to stop spending all our times in meetings, in front of the computer, or speaking with the senior executives. We have to let our employees know that we value and appreciate them and want to know what they think. We have to listen while having a quiet mind and focusing on all they have to say. We don't need to be thinking about what we are going to say. We should not be problem-solving in our minds or even thinking about what is on our to-do list.

We only retain about 25 percent of what we hear and this is because we are so busy and we don't have good listening skills.

We can learn to be better listeners and increase what we retain. There are practices that can help you be conscientious, purposeful, and intentional when listening to others and this will make a huge difference with our employees.

To maintain and earn good relationships, our employees have to know that we truly care for them. We must listen with an empathetic ear and by keeping an open mind, we can develop an energetic and enthusiastic team. When we listen to learn and understand, we are giving a gift to others.

The journey of quieting our minds, to focus better on others, and to be fully present when listening, will greatly improve our effectiveness as a manager.

CONCLUSION

Thank for making it through to the end of *Manager: How to be Successful in Your New Position*, let's hope it was informative and able to provide you with all of the tools you need to achieve your goals whatever it may be.

The next step is to take everything you have learned and make yourself the best manager you can be. Being a manager doesn't mean you have to turn into a grump and not talk with the people you used to work alongside. Rise up and show your employees, company, and world that you are the same person. You are just a better form of you.

Finally, if you found this book useful in any way, a review on Amazon is always appreciated!